Paula.

CHART TOPPERS

IMP's Top 20 Best Selling BALLADS

CONTENTS

Exclusive distributors:
International Music Publications Limited: Southend Road, Woodford Green, Essex IG8 8HN
International Music Publications GmbH Germany: Marstallstrasse 8, D-80539 München, Germany
Nuova Carisch S.p.a. - Italy: Via Campania 12, 20098 San Guiliano Milanese, Milano, Italy
Nuova Carisch S.p.a. - France: 25 rue d'hauteville, 75010 Paris, France
Nuova Carisch S.p.a. - Spain: Magallenes 25, 28015 Madrid, Spain
Danmusik: Vognmagergade 7, DK-1120 Copenhagen K, Denmark

Production: Miranda Steel

Published 1998

Because You Loved Me

Words and Music by
DIANE WARREN

4

Everything I Do
(I Do It For You)

Words and Music by
BRYAN ADAMS, ROBERT JOHN "MUTT" LANGE
and MICHAEL KAMEN

VERSE 2:
Look into your heart
You will find there's nothin' there to hide
Take me as I am, take my life
I would give it all, I would sacrifice.

Don't tell me it's not worth fightin' for
I can't help it, there's nothin' I want more
You know it's true, everything I do
I do it for you.

Eternal Flame

Words and Music by
BILLY STEINBERG, TOM KELLY
and SUSANNA HOFFS

14

The Greatest Love Of All

Words by LINDA CREED
Music by MICHAEL MASSER

1.3. I be -lieve the chil — dren are our fu — ture;
be. 2. Ev - ery-bod - y's search - ing for a he - ro;

teach them well and let__them lead__the way.
peo -ple need some-one__to look up_____ to.

Show them all the beau - ty they pos -sess in -
I nev - er found an - y -one who ful -filled my

18

Hero

Words and Music by
WALTER AFANASIEFF and MARIAH CAREY

How Do I Live

Words and Music by
DIANE WARREN

now how do I, oh, how do I live

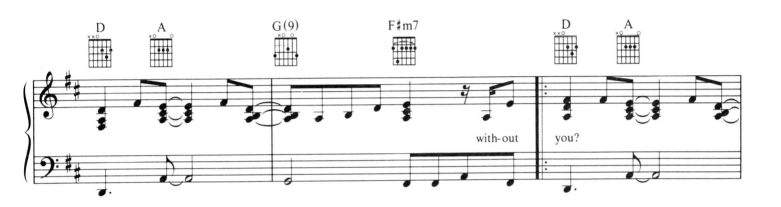

with-out you?

Repeat ad lib. and fade
(vocal 1st time only)

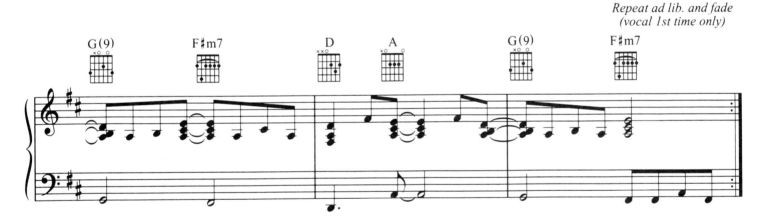

Verse 2:
Without you, there'd be no sun in my sky,
There would be no love in my life,
There'd be no world left for me.
And I, baby, I don't know what I would do,
I'd be lost if I lost you.
If you ever leave,
Baby, you would take away everything real in my life.
And tell me now...
(To Chorus:)

Forever Love

Words and Music by
GARY BARLOW

Ooh,_____ oh __ yeah,_

well I feel._____

I Will Always Love You

Words and Music by
DOLLY PARTON

36

Verse 3: Instrumental solo

Verse 4:
I hope life treats you kind
And I hope you have all you've dreamed of.
And I wish to you, joy and happiness.
But above all this, I wish you love.
(To Chorus:)

My Heart Will Go On

Words by WILL JENNINGS
Music by JAMES HORNER

44

The Power Of Love

Words by JENNIFER RUSH and MARY SUSAN APPLEGATE
Music by CANDY DE ROUGE and GUNTHER MENDE

The whis-pers___ in the morn-ing___ of lov-ers sleep-ing tight,

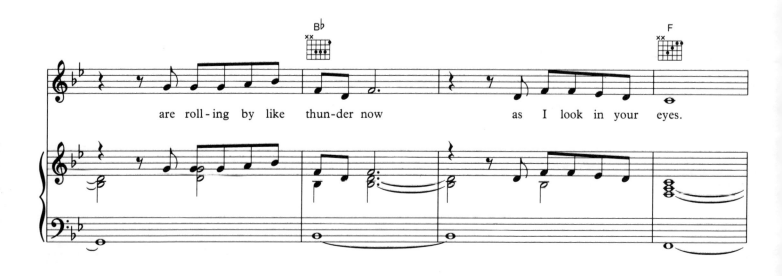

are roll-ing by like thun-der now as I look in your eyes.

I hold on to your bo-dy,___
times,_____
and feel each move you
it seems I'm far a-

51

Promise Me

Words and Music by
BEVERLEY CRAVEN

Put Your Arms Around Me

Words and Music by
JOHN McELHONE, SHARLEEN SPITERI,
ROBERT HODGENS and DAVE STEWART

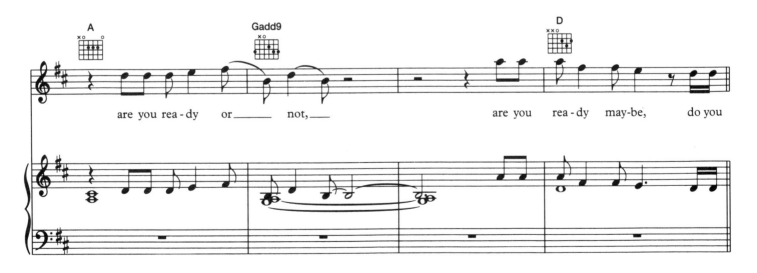

60

The Rose

Words and Music by
AMANDA McBROOM

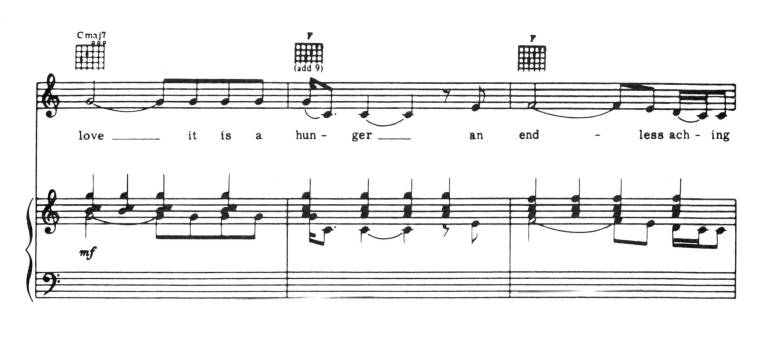

love _____ it is a hun - ger _____ an end - less ach - ing

need. _____ I say _ love it is a flow - er _____ and

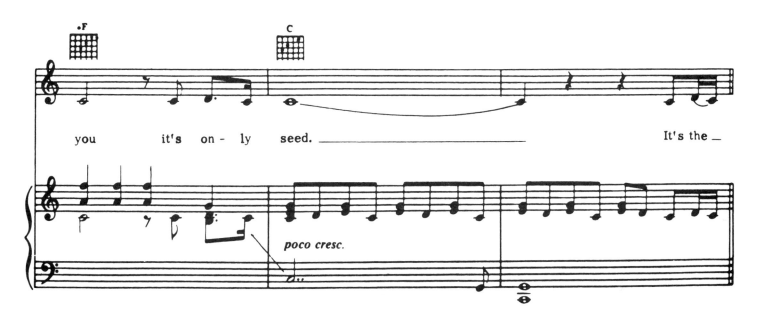

you it's on - ly seed. _____ It's the _

64

Something About The Way
You Look Tonight

Words by BERNIE TAUPIN
Music by ELTON JOHN

There was a

time____ I was ev-ery-thing and no-thing all in one.____

When you found me____ I was feel-ing like a cloud a-cross the sun.____

Un-Break My Heart

Words and Music by
DIANE WARREN

Somewhere My Love

Words by PAUL FRANCIS WEBSTER
Music by MAURICE JARRE

Tell Him

Words and Music by
LINDA THOMPSON, DAVID FOSTER and WALTER AFANASIEFF

Verse 2:
(Barbra:)
Touch him with the gentleness you feel inside. (C: I feel it.)
Your love can't be denied.
The truth will set you free.
You'll have what's meant to be.
All in time, you'll see.
(Celine:)
I love him, (B: Then show him.)
Of that much I can be sure. (B: Hold him close to you.)
I don't think I could endure
If I let him walk away
When I have so much to say.
(To Chorus:)

When A Man Loves A Woman

Words and Music by
CALVIN LEWIS and **ANDREW WRIGHT**

The Wind Beneath My Wings

Words and Music by
LARRY HENLEY and **JEFF SILBAR**

You've Got A Friend

Slowly, with expression

Words and Music by
CAROLE KING

When you're down ____ and trou - bled and you need ____
a - bove ____ you grows dark ____

some love and care, ____ and ____ noth - in', ____
and full of clouds, ____ and that ol' ____ north wind ____